What's in this booklet?

Helping yourself – advice for parents 2

Your own feelings 2

Helping your children 2

Grieving together 4

Life without your partner 4

When a parent experiences the death of a child 5

A special mention for brothers and sisters 5

Helping your children 6

Grief in families 6

Talking about death 6

Coping with a death – the first weeks 8

Telling children that a parent or sibling has died 8

Accidents and other sudden deaths 8

Traumatic stress 10

Telling the story of what happened 10

Seeing the body and attending the funeral 11

Supporting a child who has been bereaved
    through suicide 14

Family life – the first year 15

Exploring and sharing feelings 15

Changes in behaviour 15

How children grieve 16

School 20

Anniversaries, birthdays and other special days 21

When should I get professional help? 21

Practical ways to support children 23

Expressing emotions: jar of memories 24

Treasuring memories: memory box 26

Exploring feelings: biscuit feeling faces 28

Email Us 29

Online Tools 30

Sources of information and support 31

Useful reading 32

Helping yourself – advice for parents

Your own feelings

It is important to remember that people react differently when they experience a death. How someone reacts to a death is highly personal and depends on many different factors. Some of these factors are age, personality, coping style, relationships, past experiences, religious beliefs and cultural background. It is quite common for members of the same family to react in different ways even though they have experienced the death of the same person. While shock is a common reaction at first, some may not show any visible reactions, while others may show their distress by crying, for example.

Coping with your own feelings after someone has died can be especially difficult when you are trying to support your child or children. People tend to experience a range of intense emotions. You may feel shocked, sad, angry, guilty, anxious, relieved, lonely, irritable and many other feelings. Indeed, you may feel a number of these emotions all at the same time and find it hard to sort out and express what you feel. Or you may be aware that you feel intense sadness that things will never be the same again and that you will never be able to do the things you had planned. Everyday situations and tasks can feel impossible to achieve. Relating to other people can become a great strain.

Such reactions are natural after a death. In order to support your children well, you will need to make efforts to look after yourself first. This will include making time for yourself to experience your own feelings of grief.

You may find family and friends provide the support you need. Sometimes, though, it can help to talk to someone more neutral or others in a similar situation. If you feel you could benefit from some support it might help to discuss this with your family doctor or call the Winston's Wish helpline to find out about local support services (see page 31).

Helping your children

Children, too, react in different ways to the death of someone important. This booklet gives some information about the normal grief reactions that children and young people may go through. It also aims to give ideas about how parents can support their children. It can be hard to know you've found the right words so we include some suggestions about what parents might say to children at different times and in different situations.

You will be able to support your children most effectively when you look after yourself. This can seem like an impossible task when you're feeling overwhelmed by your grief and aware, at the same time, that your children need you. However, getting outside support will make sure that you can respond confidently to both the physical and emotional needs of your children. Outside support can sometimes mean professional support (see page 21), or it can mean leaning on family and friends, or it can mean giving yourself permission to take time to feel the feelings that follow after the death of someone important.

Children often look to their parents to see how they are expected to react when someone has died. It is not going to damage your children if you cry in front of them or with them. It can be helpful if you give a simple explanation such as: "Mum's feeling sad and crying because dad died. I really miss him." Saying things out loud helps children to understand and be more aware of what is happening in their world. It is more helpful and reassuring to children if you show your feelings rather than pretending that everything is all right. Children are sensitive to what's going on around them, and they pick up on feelings and atmosphere within the family. They are therefore likely to worry or blame themselves if things are kept from them. They may think they shouldn't talk about the person who died or show their feelings. This makes grieving more complicated and can lead to other problems.

"As a bereaved parent I only want to do what is best for my children and myself. But it is very difficult to cope with my own loss as well as the great loss the children have had." Maria

Grieving together

Life without your partner

When a husband, wife or partner dies it is normal to feel lost. Some people have said they feel like a part of them is missing and that they don't know who they are any more. Perhaps one of the hardest things is adjusting to life as a lone parent. This is a challenging adjustment as in many families partners balance each other, back each other up and often make joint decisions about everyday family life.

Many people faced with being a lone parent because of a bereavement can feel overwhelmed at first. In the short term there will, of course, be disruption to normal family routines and things may be a bit unfocused. As time goes on, children will do better if routines and boundaries are in place and enforced. Taking life one step at a time – and being clear, consistent and confident about decisions affecting your children – will help you and your children deal with your loss.

"After our son Ben died, our 4-year-old daughter kept asking if she could go to visit him and God. Her older brother got angry and said 'no God would have let this happen!' and he kept shouting at his sister for asking such stupid questions. We just didn't know what to say." Sarah and Dan

When a parent experiences the death of a child

The death of a child is one of the hardest, if not the hardest, things a couple or a parent can face in life. You never expect to live longer than your children.

You may find it hard to talk to your family and friends or your partner. However, some couples have said that the experience has brought them closer together as they've had to rely on each other and show their vulnerabilities in ways they had not done before.

Many parents find they cope differently to their partner and this can cause considerable strain in a relationship. However, it can be helpful if you have different strategies and ideas that might work for each other at different times. Accepting difference is sometimes difficult at the best of times so it's normal to struggle with difference when you are dealing with the loss of your child.

A special mention for brothers and sisters

It is quite common for bereaved children to experience feelings of guilt associated with being alive when their sibling has died. Guilt can also follow from a child's worry that their 'death wishes' may have caused the tragedy.

Children benefit from being reassured that their sibling's death was not their fault. It is natural for parents to struggle with being available to their surviving children when they are dealing with their own grief. However, children are more able to manage changes when they are given clear information about what is happening and why. Getting reassurance will help reduce their worries. If their worries are addressed early on they have a greater chance of not being overwhelmed by them.

Children in this situation often benefit from meeting other children who have experienced the death of a sibling so they can talk with others who understand how they are feeling.

"I thought it was because I was riding my bike too far ahead that the lorry hit my sister." Harry

Helping your children

"I tried not to cry in front of her and then I wondered why she didn't seem upset that her mum had died. Things were easier when we told each other we cried in private. Now we share our grief." Judith

Grief in families

Family members often try to protect each other. This complicated and normal emotional balancing act means that family members might react differently to a death. Similarly, at different times they may be feeling very different things. Individual family members often unconsciously try to balance each other out – when one person is sad, another might try to support them by appearing cheerful. At other times the roles may be reversed. This is what we call the 'protection racket'. It is done with the best of intentions, and is normal in families, but it sometimes makes it difficult for family members to be open about their grief because they are scared of upsetting each other.

Childhood is often thought to be a time when children should be free from difficulties and challenging life events. In reality this is seldom possible and major life events such as serious illness and death happen all too frequently to many families. Many parents feel they want to protect their children when a death happens. They think that by not talking about it their children will not be affected and will therefore not need to worry. However, it can often be more helpful to talk about what is happening so that children feel included and valued.

Talking about death

Not talking about important issues can be harder than talking about them.

Many people understandably worry about talking to children and young people about death. They might worry about what to say, about saying the wrong thing, or being asked questions they feel they can't answer. The easiest way to talk to children and young people is to be direct, clear and honest. When children are not told things they can feel left out and are often confused by lack of information. Sometimes this can result in them blaming themselves for what happened.

It is often easier for children if they are given information in small chunks, rather than all in one go, and simple messages often need to be repeated several times. Any suggested words given in this booklet will therefore need to be adapted to suit the individual situations and the age of each individual child. It is not a question of being brutally frank: what is important is to explain things in language that children can understand.

"I now realise that everyone in the family is different. At first I thought Andrew didn't care, he was so manic and hyper, but eventually he told me he was trying to be strong for my sake." Susan

Coping with a death – the first weeks

"It was so hard to tell her that her father had died. But I wanted her to realise that this wasn't something like being away on one of his business trips." Jane

Telling children that a parent or sibling has died

This may be the hardest thing you have ever had to do.

You might say something like: "Remember I told you mum was ill, so ill the doctors couldn't make her better. I have something very sad to tell you. Mum died this morning."

It is best to say 'died' than to use words like 'gone to sleep', 'passed away' or 'lost', as these can be confusing for children. A child who is told that 'mummy has gone away' may expect her to return as she has in the past when the same words have been used. And if someone has been 'lost', this could mean to a 4-year-old that they might be 'found' again, or if they are 'asleep' that they can wake up. Though many adults often find it hard to use the word 'died', it is easier for children to understand. They will value your honesty and a trusting relationship will allow them to talk openly to you in the future.

It is impossible to predict how children will take the news and their reactions may range from great distress to not seeming to be bothered. They may say: "What's

for tea?" or "Can I go to the shops now?" These are very normal reactions and do not mean that the child is uncaring.

Sometimes children and adults are comforted by the idea of heaven or a similar place where someone is no longer ill. Your own beliefs will help you to decide whether or not to talk to children about such things and how to describe them.

Accidents and other sudden deaths

Accidents, such as car accidents, can be hard to believe because they happen so suddenly. One minute the person was alive and the next they have died. It helps to explain to children about the accident, what happened, what injuries were caused, why the accident happened and that the person has died. Doing this will help to fill in some of the missing information that can cause worries and doubts.

Parents can tell children about the accident perhaps using words like: "I have something sad to tell you about dad. Today when he was going to work there was a car accident and he died. The other driver was going very fast, and we think this caused the accident. Dad's car and another car hit each other on the road and crashed. Dad hit his head when the car crashed and the bang on the head was so hard that he died".

Where there is no known cause for the accident, it can help to say: "We don't really know what caused the accident. There are lots of reasons why it might have happened, like someone not concentrating or swerving to avoid something on the road. But we don't really know what caused this accident. Sometimes accidents just happen".

In some cases, where there has been an accident, it might be especially helpful for family members, including children, to see the body and go to the funeral. This can help them to understand the reality of the situation. (Seeing the body and funerals are discussed more on page 11.)

Joe, do you remember I told you mummy was ill – so ill the doctors couldn't make her better? I have something very sad to tell you. Last night she found it hard to breathe and mummy died this morning.

The policeman said she died as soon as the accident happened. The ambulance came but her heart had stopped forever.

Traumatic stress

When someone dies suddenly, and in traumatic circumstances, family members sometimes show signs of traumatic stress. This might include having unwanted pictures or images of the trauma (often called flashbacks) coming into your mind, or upsetting dreams. This can happen even if you didn't actually see what happened but were told later.

You may also experience distressing physical reactions: these might include symptoms such as the heart beating faster and dizziness. These are all normal reactions and will usually lessen in intensity over time. Just how long this will take will be different for different people. However, if you or your children are affected by such signs and symptoms, or find it difficult to get off to sleep or stay asleep, or feel detached from others, then it might be time to seek support. The Winston's Wish helpline is one option or you may prefer to speak with your family doctor. It is important to remember and to tell your children that, with help, things can be different.

Telling the story of what happened

In the work we do with children, we sometimes give them blank pages which look like the frames from rolls of film. Children are encouraged to think about what life was like before the person died, what happened the day before the death, to describe the death, what happened during the next day or days, and what life is like now. Children may either draw pictures or write down words to tell their story: they are encouraged to draw

Here a child carefully draws the sequence of events which led up to a road traffic accident in which they witnessed the death of their parent.

out their understanding of what happened frame by frame. They are later encouraged to think of the film as a video which can be rewound and the tape put away. For children struggling with intrusive images it can give them a sense of mastery over the continual replaying of traumatic images.

Seeing the body and attending the funeral

Some families believe that children should not see someone's body after they have died or attend the funeral. However, it can help children to begin to accept the reality of the death, and also to be less scared. Children are usually more scared about what they don't know than what they are allowed to be part of as this enables them to feel more included.

Involvement in rituals following a death will, of course, vary in families depending on their cultural and religious beliefs, but it can help children if they can see for themselves rather than let their imaginations run riot. Some families will be clear about whether they wish children to see the body or not, but if they are not sure then it sometimes helps if children can make up their own minds. To do this, they need to know a bit about what it will be like.

Some ideas about what you could say about seeing the body

Sometimes, when someone dies, family and friends go and see the body of the person who has died to say goodbye. Dad's body is in a big box called a coffin. Because he has died, his body is the bit that is left. What is special about him – his spirit and the memories we have of him – these will last for ever. We soon need to say goodbye to his body and then bury or cremate him. That's why we are going to have a funeral. Before the funeral though you might want to go and see him.

If the child says 'yes', check before they go that they still want to. Tell the child that it is all right to go up close to the body and to touch or kiss the person's body, or to keep their distance and look from the door.

His body won't be like it used to be. Because he has died he can't talk or walk or sleep. He doesn't need to eat. His body might feel cold and a bit like wax. Would you like to go and see his body?

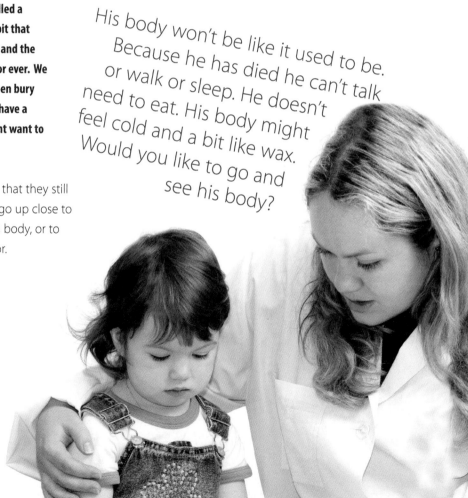

If the child says 'no', reassure them that it is all right and that sometimes grown ups don't want to go and see the person after they have died. Check out that the child hasn't changed their mind. You may want to suggest that they can make a card or picture which can be put in the coffin for them. Sometimes a child might choose two identical objects, such as a soft toy. They send one to be put into the coffin, and keep one for themselves or to put in their memory box (see page 26).

Dad's body will be in a box similar to this. It's called a coffin.

Some ideas about what you could say about attending the funeral

Again, families sometimes have set views about what should happen, but it helps to give the child enough information to choose. You might say something like:

When someone dies we have a special service called a funeral. The service is often held in a special place (church, chapel, synagogue or mosque) and is a time for people to say goodbye to the person who has died and to be with their family.

At the funeral there might be songs and prayers and people saying what they remember about the person who has died.

On Thursday we are having dad's funeral. His body will be there in a special box called a coffin and many of dad's family and friends will be there. Some of them may be very upset and may be crying. After the funeral dad's body in the coffin will be buried/burnt. Would you like to go to dad's funeral?

Reassure the child that cremation cannot hurt the person who has died and that dead bodies do not feel pain.

If the child says 'yes', check out nearer the time that the child still wants to go and make sure that someone, such as a family friend, is there to keep a special eye on them. Give them detailed information about what to expect at the funeral. They may also want to contribute to planning the service as well as doing something like providing a poem to be read out.

If the child says 'no', remember that children have a habit of changing their minds, so check out a little later that they still don't want to go. Try to think of other ways they can participate in the service: they could perhaps write a letter, their thoughts or a poem, or draw a picture or put something in the coffin. It can also help a child who does not want to attend the funeral to go and see the flowers or visit the grave later in the day, or for someone to take photographs of the flowers or grave.

"He said he wanted to be involved and he wrote the most beautiful poem about his father and helped with the prayers at the funeral." Rita

"How do you tell a child their mum has died and that she decided to end it all? It didn't seem fair to burden her with it, but then again I thought, above all, she now needed to be able to trust me completely." Ed

Supporting a child who has been bereaved through suicide

Explaining to a child that someone has died by suicide is possibly one of the most difficult situations that a parent or carer might ever face. *Beyond the Rough Rock* offers practical advice for families in the immediate days and weeks when suicide has been the cause of death. It is a useful booklet aimed at giving parents and professionals the confidence to involve children in discussions about the nature of a death by suicide. It is hoped that children may then begin to understand some of the complexities that often surround suicide. The booklet includes child-friendly activities to do as a family as they begin to make sense of what has happened and start to look at ways in which they can learn to cope.

The title of the booklet – *Beyond the Rough Rock* – is taken from an activity that we call 'rocky rocks'. A 'rough rock' can be used to represent the difficult, hard and painful memories we sometimes have. All too often a family suicide leaves behind such difficult memories and feelings. A 'smooth pebble' is for hope, comfort and faith in the future. And finally a beautiful 'gemstone' gives eternal life to special memories. Children need to find ways of balancing all three – so they can find their way beyond the rough rock. This activity can help people look beyond the 'rough, sharp rock' and to find a balance between the good, bad and everyday memories that are a natural part of family life.

You can order this booklet from our website at shop.winstonswish.org

Winston's Wish
the charity for bereaved children

beyond the
rough rock
Supporting a child who has been bereaved through suicide

Family life – the first year

Exploring and sharing feelings

All people, whether young or older, have many intense feelings when someone dies. People often feel sad, confused, angry, guilty and sometimes even relief if the person who died had been poorly for some time or if they had a difficult relationship with them.

Children are just the same but, depending on their age and stage of development, their ability to understand and use words to describe their feelings varies. It helps to talk with children about how they are feeling and to talk about the feelings people normally have when someone important in their life dies. With very young children it is often easier to do this using some of their own soft toys, puppets or dolls.

Changes in behaviour

It can be helpful to remember that children's experience of a death in the family, and their reactions to it, may be different to yours as an adult. Children often show their feelings about many things through their behaviour, and bereavement is no exception. Their behaviour will correspond to their age and understanding of what has happened.

Initial reactions to news of a death may range from great distress to what may seem like a lack of concern. Your child may find it impossible to speak, they may be unable to stop crying or they may ask: "What are we having for dinner?" When first told of the death, younger children may be mainly concerned with the 'when' and 'where' of the death. Slightly older children may also want to know the 'how' and older children and young people will also explore the 'why'. All of these reactions – and more – are natural reactions and do not mean that your child doesn't care or is over-reacting.

While most children experience their grief differently to adults, this is even more so for younger children. We often talk of children 'puddle jumping' or 'jumping in and out of puddles of grief' to describe the grieving process of children.

"At school I punched the desk and threw books. I was so angry. I hated everything and everybody. They all seemed so happy."
Josh

"I think daddy will come back for my birthday." Bethany

Older children and adults tend not to move in and out of their grief so quickly. However, this difference doesn't mean that they care any less or are less affected by what has happened.

Children are often talked about as behaving badly or behaving well. Many people think bereaved children will react by behaving badly and, though this can be true, many children also behave 'very well' by throwing themselves into their school work and helping around the house, believing that if they are very good things might be different at home. Although difficult behaviour is most often seen as a sign that a child would benefit from support, it is important that the well-behaved child is not overlooked. Some children become very withdrawn, not wanting to talk or do anything, but because they are quiet and don't cause trouble their needs can go relatively unnoticed. Other children struggle in more visible ways and show their feelings by getting into squabbles and fights, having outbursts and temper tantrums. Sometimes children will be clingy and are worried that their surviving parent will also die. It helps children to be told who would look after them

if you were ill or were to die, while reassuring them that, as far as you are aware, you are well and unlikely to die.

Helping children talk about the person who died helps them to understand and cope with what is happening in their family. Remember that it is not unusual or uncommon for a child's behaviour to be different at home than it is at school. Keeping the lines of communication open with school is important so that problems can be discussed before they get out of hand.

How children grieve

The age of a child has a direct impact on their level of understanding about what has happened. As a child gets older their ability to understand about death and dying increases. To help you feel more confident about what to explain about the death – and how – it is helpful and necessary to first appreciate what children know about death and what they are capable of learning at the various stages of their development.

Children under 2 years old

Very young children and babies are not able to understand death. They experience the loss as a separation from someone they have an attachment to. And although children at this age do not have much language to express their loss they will react to it. They may search for the person who died, they may cry inconsolably or be withdrawn.

Children this age will also be affected by the emotional state of other important people in their lives. They will respond to a steady, loving, interesting environment which will enable them to continue to thrive. As the child grows, so will their ability to understand and use speech to express themselves and so there will be opportunities to talk about the person who died and help them build their own story. When a child this young experiences the death of a parent it is particularly important that they are helped to know about the person.

Children aged 2 to 5

Children aged between 2 and 5 years think that death is reversible and that people who have died can come back. Children can be convinced that it was something they said or did or thought that caused the person to die. The flip side of this thinking is that they can believe their words, actions or thoughts can bring the dead person back.

They need to be reassured repeatedly that the death was not their fault. They also need clear, direct, simple explanations. Use words such as 'mummy has died' and give specific explanations about why the person died. Don't be afraid to be honest and tell your child if you don't have an answer.

It is not unusual for children of this age to revert to behaviour patterns they had when they were younger, such as bed-wetting, use of a security blanket or thumb sucking. Try to be tolerant. In time, these earlier behaviour patterns will probably disappear again, once family life resumes.

"Last night I dreamed that my mum came to meet me from school: she hugged me and gave me the softest blanket ever to wrap round because she thought I was cold." Matthew

"I have all these feelings building up inside me and sometimes I just explode."

Chris

One of the most difficult aspects of a child's grief at these ages is how they ask the same questions over and over again in an effort to begin making sense of their loss. Children are naturally curious and they want to make sense of what is happening in their world. Their repeated questions are not a sign that your explanations aren't good enough – it is just the way they do things at this age. Reading books on death and loss, playing, drawing and giving them opportunities to identify and talk about worries and feelings will all help them deal with the loss. When they experience a death in this age range they are at their most helpless and are most dependent on adults to regain their balance.

Children aged 6 to 9

In this age range children begin to develop an understanding of death as irreversible and something that will happen to all living things but they may be confused about it. It is not uncommon for children to think of death as something spooky, like a zombie or a spirit that comes to get you. It is important that their specific worries are spoken about, that they share bad dreams and are told that what they're feeling is normal. Children are reassured by having their worrying and negative thoughts talked through, giving them the skills and confidence to be in charge of them.

Children may display what you feel is an unhealthy curiosity with issues such as what a dead body looks like and what happens to a body after a person has been dead for some time. This curiosity is natural and they will benefit from clear explanations. They may worry about how the person who has died will eat, breathe and keep warm. It is important to give them information and tell them that once someone has died, the body doesn't feel any more and they don't get hungry.

Children at this stage may complain of a sore tummy, headaches or just generally not feeling well. These are what we call 'somatic' complaints, where unexpressed feelings and emotions can lead to physical symptoms or discomfort. Somatic complaints are normal but it is important that routines are maintained while gently acknowledging that it hurts when someone important dies.

Children this age may have difficulty expressing feelings verbally and may retreat into themselves. In dealing with their feelings of helplessness, you may notice increased aggression. It is important to avoid clichés such as: "You're such a brave boy/girl". Children will interpret this to mean that you want or need them not to share their feelings. They need you and other important people in their lives to show them that it is OK to express their feelings.

Children aged 10 to 13

In this age range children are much more aware of the finality of death and the impact the death has on them. They are able to understand death as both concrete and abstract.

Children may experience difficulties in their interactions with their peers. The death of someone important can make them feel different at the very time that they want to be the same as everyone else.

It is important to find ways to build their self-esteem. Children at this age are beginning to think of the longer term consequences of the loss of the relationship. They are aware of the loss they feel in the present but also of the losses they will experience in the coming months and years when they encounter certain important milestones or occasions and realise that they won't be able to share these with the person who has died.

At this age children are beginning to move away from dependence on the family and they start to form important relationships with other children. The death of someone important can easily destabilise them, leaving them feeling unsafe and more dependent on the family. Their ability to manage their feelings may be disrupted and can lead to mood swings or more definite ups and downs in their feelings. Big emotional releases (such as anger or distress) are not uncommon but can be scary for children at this stage. They will benefit from your willingness to listen and your assurances that the feelings are normal.

Adolescents

Friends and peers are increasingly important as young people develop their ideas of who they are and what is important to them. They want to be accepted by other important people in their lives. Their bodies are changing, they are aware of all sorts of possibilities for themselves and are more aware of the future – their future. It is quite common for risk-taking behaviour to increase during adolescence as young people test the boundaries.

They may struggle to make longer term plans as the death of someone important causes them to reflect on 'the meaning of life' and ponder on the question "What's the point?" Or you may find they are so busy with different activities that they don't stop to reflect. This can be an effective way of keeping intense feelings under wraps if they are worried about losing control of their emotions.

If you notice a teenager who is withdrawing, acting very matter of fact and detached, or angry and protesting, then

"The first time I cried was several months later. I was at a friend's house after school. She wasn't feeling well and her mum brought her a glass of milk. Suddenly I realised that my mum was never going to do that again." Emma

"When they heard what had happened, all the children in class asked to send notes home to Michael. Some even shared their own experiences of loss; they said they missed Michael and wanted him back in goal! He read their notes and decided to come back to school the next day. I guess he knew they cared about his dad's death, but importantly he also knew he would be treated as normal." Tim, a teacher

remain available for them – but don't push. Your job is to remind them that you're there and that if they would prefer to speak to someone else you'll help them find peers or other trusted adults to support them. Although an adolescent's grieving process is most like an adult's, they are still going through important emotional development at this age and are not ready to manage adult responsibilities even if at times they think they are adult. They need to be reassured of your love and support and to know that the limits you set are still enforced.

School

School provides a familiar, routine part of children's lives. Many children who have been bereaved find going to school helpful, even the day after someone has died, because it shows that even though other things in their lives are changing, some things are reliable and stay the same.

It is normal for bereaved children to find it hard to concentrate at school for a while. If this persists, or if the child refuses to go to school, it often helps to go and talk to the child's teacher to discuss ways in which help can be offered.

Parents and children who have experienced a death can worry about returning to school and telling people what has happened. Schools are usually willing to help families when they have experienced a bereavement. Keeping the lines of communication open means that staff and families can help each other to support the child.

It helps to tell the school as soon as possible after the death (and, if the death is expected, to inform them before the person has died). By telling the school, staff can help your child to cope with what has happened.

A school is part of the community and therefore can initiate accurate information that can help to stop rumours that might be circulating. Many parents find they receive a great deal of support from other parents when there has been such an open attitude.

Children often tease each other about being different. A bereavement is no exception. With the child's permission, it can help if the teacher sits down with the child and their peers and tells them what has happened. The teacher can try to explain how the child might be feeling and encourage friends to be openly supportive. When this happens, peers are usually genuinely concerned and this reduces the risk of the child feeling ashamed and embarrassed.

When someone important in a child's life dies there are many times throughout the year when memories are particularly vivid. Events like Christmas, birthdays, Mother's or Father's Day are obvious, but it can be other days, such as the anniversary of the death or a school leavers' evening, that can be difficult too.

It can help if the teacher and child sit down together and make a list of all the important dates throughout the year when the child might particularly be thinking about the person who has died. It can act as a reminder to the teacher to check out how the child is feeling on that day. This is a useful document which can be shared by the teaching staff. It can also be helpful to make a simple family tree: again, this can be given to all the staff who teach the bereaved child. These are simple, practical ideas that tell the child that their school understands the importance of a family bereavement. As a parent, you may well need to suggest this to your child's teacher. Teachers and other professionals are often worried about saying anything in case they make matters worse. However, it is silence that usually makes matters worse!

Anniversaries, birthdays and other special days

Special days such as birthdays and anniversaries can be very hard after someone important in a family has died. Families can feel as though they do not want to celebrate or even to recognise the event. Children can find this especially hard.

It does help to try and plan these days, to prepare openly for a day you know is going to be challenging. Some families find it helps if they continue to recognise the event but put aside a special time that day to remember the person who

has died. Some families choose to light a candle or make something for their memory box or scrapbook to mark the occasion. For example, on Christmas Day it may be that the family has its normal Christmas routine but takes time to visit the cemetery, or go to a place the person who died liked so that they can remember him or her. Many children will enjoy making a special tree decoration that can be hung on the tree each year to make sure that the person who has died is included in Christmas celebrations. Some families choose to do some of these things but not on the actual day. It is important that all family members have a choice about what they do.

When should I get professional help?

Most children and their families will be able to cope with the death of a close family member and, if families can talk about what is happening and their feelings, they cope surprisingly well. It is often when family members cannot talk to each other that they find they have more problems. So, if all else fails, try to keep talking!

Many people worry about their children and they sometimes feel they should seek professional help immediately after the death. As mentioned in the section 'How children grieve' (see page 16), it is very normal for a child not to seem to react immediately to the news of a death.

"The first Christmas was so difficult, leaving her name off the Christmas cards was incredibly hard. I was dreading Christmas without her but somehow we did get through it and as usual, Samuel loved his presents." Julian

"Making the memory jars was great fun. Mum and I had some memories which were the same and some which were different. I keep my jar safe in my memory box, mum has hers on the windowsill in the kitchen." Sophie

Frequently, however, there may be changes and a disruption of their normal sleep pattern. They may find it hard to get to sleep or have dreams about the person who has died. Appetite can also be affected: for example, the child may not want to eat or may overeat. They may react differently to daily activities and may not want to go to school or see friends.

Sometimes a bereaved child may even say they want to die so that they can be with the dead person. This is not necessarily a sign that a child will self-harm but it is important they are told that it is not possible to re-join the person who has died. They need to have an explanation that describes what death actually means while, at the same time, acknowledging the painful emotions they feel because someone important has died.

Most of these changes in behaviour will gradually disappear. However, if they persist or become severe, it might be best to seek help – in the first case through your family doctor or by telephoning our helpline to discuss your concerns further.

And finally

It is important to repeat that grief is normal, natural and necessary. It can be so hard to watch your children grieving – and tempting to try to protect them through silence. However, your willingness to acknowledge their thoughts and feelings and to keep talking about the person who has died will help them face the future with confidence and remember the person's life, rather than focus on their death.

Practical ways to support children

Here are some activities which may help your children cope with the effects of bereavement on family life, in a safe and creative way. They are simply ideas that other people have used and found helpful and you can adapt them to suit your situation. Only take the ideas on board if you feel comfortable with them. There is no 'right way' to handle a bereavement in the family. Your family is unique and you need to do things in the way that suits you all.

Expressing emotions: jar of memories   24

Treasuring memories: memory box   26

Exploring feelings: biscuit feeling faces   28

For young people: email us   29

For young people: online tools   30

Expressing emotions: jar of memories

If we do not acknowledge that someone has died, then we certainly cannot acknowledge the feelings that go with it. Some adults feel that as long as it is not given a name, or discussed, children will go on with their lives as though nothing has happened.

Children need to understand that fear, love, anger, sadness – and a whole lot more – are all appropriate feelings when a person they care about has died.

This is a way to help families express and share their feelings.

Between you, choose five feelings that feel important: for example anger, love, fear, sadness and hope. Give each feeling a colour. Then ask for examples of what thoughts or situations trigger these feelings. Here are some examples of colours, feelings and thoughts from Liam whose mum died of cancer.

The idea of a jar with layers of coloured salt can also be used to represent memories. Different colours stand for different memories of the person who has died.

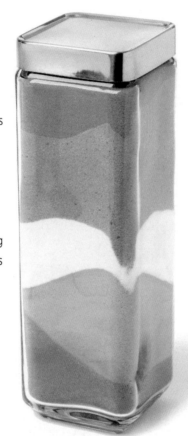

Red "My mum wore these really big bright red earrings when she went out in the evenings."

Blue "We had this old blanket from when I was a baby that she tucked around me when I felt poorly."

Yellow "The walls in the hospital were meant to cheer you up but I hated seeing her there."

Green "She was always in the garden, humming away while she weeded."

Pink "Roses were her favourite flower. She had pink roses every year on her birthday."

Jar of memories

YOU'LL NEED:

A small clean jar with a screw-top lid
Packet of table salt
Coloured chalks or pastels
Cotton wool ball
Five pieces of A4 paper and one small piece of paper

WHAT TO DO:

Each different colour in your jar of memories will represent a thought or feeling that you have had since someone in your family died. Whether happy or sad, they are important feelings to you.

Step 1: Think about five feelings you have.

Step 2: Begin by thinking of one thought that goes with each of the five feelings. Write these down on the small piece of paper.

Step 3: Decide on a colour for each feeling and mark that colour next to the feeling on your paper.

Step 4: Fill a small jar right up to the brim with salt, making sure it is jammed full. This gives you the exact amount of salt needed. Then tip the salt out of the jar into five piles on the five pieces of paper. Each of these piles will represent a feeling, so you could make them equal in size, or if some feelings are more significant, put more salt in that pile.

Step 5: Pick a coloured chalk or pastel and start to rub it into one pile of salt. As you rub it in, the salt will begin to turn that colour. Keep rubbing in a circular motion until it is the colour you want – the longer you rub, the stronger the colour.

Step 6: Once you have coloured all five piles of salt, carefully tip them into the jar. You can do this in straight layers, or diagonal ones, in thin strips or large ones – it is up to you. Once you have finished, tap the jar gently to settle the contents and add more salt if necessary. Then put a cotton wool ball on top and screw the lid back on tightly. The cotton wool ball stops the colours from mixing up as it forms a good seal.

Step 7: Share your jar with someone you feel safe with; tell them what the colours mean to you.

Step 8: Decide where you will keep your jar to remind you of all your different feelings.

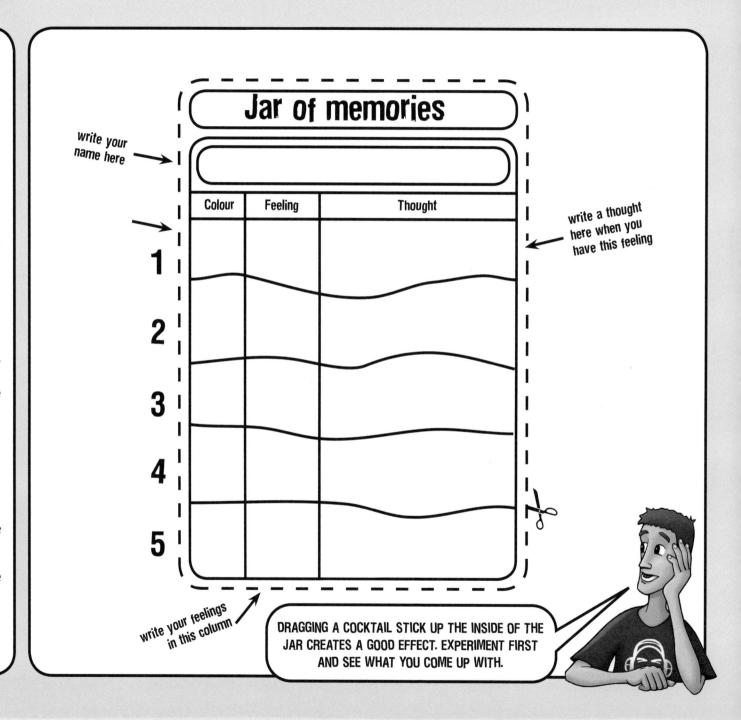

Treasuring memories: memory box

Children and young people need help to build and hold on to positive memories. Sometimes it can help to keep special things connected with the person who died in a safe place, like a box, which children can add to whenever they want and can show to other people if they want to. You can use a shoe box or a biscuit tin or buy memory boxes specially made by Winston's Wish.

Depending on the age of the child or young person, this may be an activity they prefer to do alone or one they would prefer to do with an adult – a parent, grandparent or family friend. Those close to the child could add labels that prompt stories attached to the objects; these stories will mean a lot to children in the future.

All sorts of things can be collected that trigger memories of the person who died including tickets from places visited together, jewellery, cards, feathers found on a special walk, shells from a beach holiday, certificates and so on. A bottle of aftershave or perfume that a parent or sibling used can be included and the child encouraged to spray it on a soft toy or even themselves. Our sense of smell is one of the most powerful ways to access memories so this can evoke strong feelings of connection with their parent.

This is dad's aftershave. You like a drop or two on your pillow when you're missing him most.

We picked up this shell when we crept out and walked on the beach at midnight. Do you remember the toast and hot chocolate we had afterwards?

The story about dad gett. stuck on the roof with Mia

Memory box

YOU'LL NEED:
A box with a lid
Some things to remind you of the person who died

YOU COULD ALSO USE:
Tape
Glue
Pens
Things to personalise the outside of your box

WHAT TO DO:
In a memory box you can keep and treasure all kinds of things that remind you of the person who died. You can customise it to make it more personal, and fill it with photos, letters and objects that remind you of your experiences together.

Step 1: Find a box. It can be any type of box – it just has to be big enough for everything you want to keep in it.

Step 2: Decorate the box. You could use wrapping paper, pictures cut out of magazines, photos, stickers, shells or paints… be creative!

Step 3: Once the box is decorated, start filling it. You can put anything you want in it (as long as it will fit!) Check with other people in your family that it is OK with them for you to have things like photos and objects that belonged to the person. Below are a few ideas of some things that you could include – but don't stop there – there's loads more.

Ideas for things to put in your memory box

Photos	Postcards from holidays
CD of music	Jewellery
Perfume or aftershave	Items of clothing
Cards	Shells, cones, feathers
Letters	

Here are some ideas for things to put in your memory box:

THINK CAREFULLY ABOUT WHAT YOU PUT IN. MAKE SURE THERE ARE STORIES AND MEMORIES ATTACHED TO EACH ITEM. FOR EXAMPLE, AN OLD CINEMA TICKET MIGHT REMIND YOU OF YOUR FIRST TRIP TO THE CINEMA TOGETHER.

Biscuit feeling faces

YOU'LL NEED:
Biscuits
Icing sugar
Water
Sweets and cake decorations

WHAT TO DO:
Step 1: Mix some icing sugar with a little water to make a thick glue.

Step 2: Use the icing sugar 'glue' to stick sweets and cake decorations onto the biscuits.

Here are some ideas. See if you can spot the following...
Angry Ant
Confused Cat
Worried Warthog
Fed-up Frog
Busy Bee

Exploring feelings:
biscuit feeling faces

Children can sometimes feel overwhelmed by the range and strength of feelings they experience when someone has died. This simple and fun activity helps them to describe these feelings and understand that they are natural expressions of grief.

Ask the child to think about all the different feelings they have had since the special person in their life died. Suggest that you can make different faces for all the different feelings people have when they are grieving.

For young people: email us

It is important for children and young people to have the opportunity to ask questions about their own bereavement and feelings and to receive advice and support by email from an experienced professional.

Our email service enables children and young people to do just that; they can email one of our expert professionals about anything relating to their bereavement, any questions they may have or links to any other helpful websites.

Email us

Email ask@winstonswish.org

YOU'LL NEED:
To email ask@winstonswish.org

WHAT TO DO:
Step 1: Type your email - ask any questions you would like to ask us.

Step 2: Click send! Response time is up to 48 hours

#Help2MakeSense

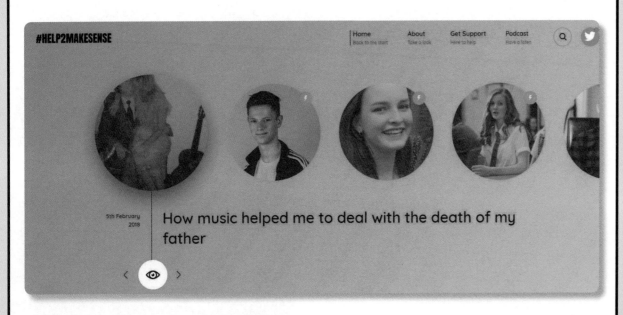

www.help2makesense.org

YOU'LL NEED:
Visit www.help2makesense.org

WHAT TO DO:
Take a look around the site, read the stories of some of the young people who have similar experiences, watch the videos, read blog posts and listen to articles.

WHAT ELSE CAN YOU DO?:
Some people may want to tell their story. If you want to share your story with other bereaved young people, please email communications@winstonswish.org

For young people: online tools

Help 2 Make Sense is an online tool brought to you by Winston's Wish. It aims to help young people who have experienced the death of a loved one come to terms with their loss. The site features a number of stories from young people who have experienced a bereavement, as well as tools and resources, such as podcasts, blog posts and more.

www.help2makesense.org

Sources of information and support

Here are some sources of support, which you may want to call on from time to time.

Winston's Wish Helpline

Information and guidance for families of bereaved children. Can provide contact details for local groups which support bereaved children. Can also provide information about a range of publications and resources including memory boxes and activity sheets.

Our free phone helpline is here to help. Every call is taken by a member of the Winston's Wish team, all of whom have professional experience of supporting bereaved children and their families. For many people who want to help a grieving child, the helpline is a vital first port of call.

As well as being a point of contact, the Winston's Wish website is itself a practical resource and support for bereaved families. Help2MakeSense.org is an online tool that aims to help young people who have experienced the death of a loved one come to terms with their loss. The site features a number of stories from young people who have experienced a bereavement, as well as tools and resources, such as podcasts, blog posts and more.

Freephone National Helpline: 08088 020 021 (Mon-Fri 9am to 5pm)
www.help2makesense.org
www.winstonswish.org

Childhood Bereavement Network

This website will help you locate services in your local area.
www.childhoodbereavementnetwork.org.uk/directory.aspx

Cruse – Bereavement Care

Telephone counselling service for those who are bereaved and those who care for bereaved people. Can offer referrals to Cruse branches and other bereavement and counselling services throughout the UK.
Day by day helpline: 0844 477 9400
Young people's helpline: 0808 808 1677
www.crusebereavementcare.org.uk
Young people's website: www.rd4u.org.uk

Samaritans

Confidential emotional support for anyone in a crisis – 24 hours a day.
Voice phone: 08457 90 90 90 (calls are charged at the local rate)
Helpline: 116 123 (24 hours, 7 days a week)
E-mail: jo@samaritans.org
www.samaritans.org

"Sometimes she just goes inside herself and I don't know what to say to her." Mary

Useful reading

For children

Muddles, Puddles and Sunshine: Your Activity Book when Someone has Died
Diana Crossley
Illustrated by Kate Sheppard
A Winston's Wish publication
Hawthorn Press, 2000
ISBN 978-1-86989058-2

This activity book offers invaluable practical and sensitive support for younger children. Beautifully illustrated, it suggests a helpful series of activities accompanied by the friendly characters Bee and Bear.

When Dinosaurs Die: A Guide to Understanding Death
Laurie Krasny Brown and Marc Brown
Time Warner Trade Publishing, 1996
ISBN 0-316-11955-5

This factual picture book uses cartoon dinosaurs to illustrate the text and comment on what is said. It is a bright and colourful book that explains death in a simple and unthreatening way. It covers many issues including "why does someone die?", "feelings about death" and "saying goodbye". It would be an excellent resource for anyone caring for young children.

For adults and families

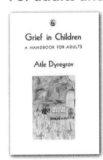

Grief in Children: A Handbook for Adults
Atle Dyregrov
Jessica Kingsley Publishers Ltd, 1991
ISBN 978-7853021138

This is a very practical and useful book written for adults to help them understand how children feel when someone important in their life dies.

Out of the Blue: Making Memories Last when Someone has Died
Julie Stokes and Paul Oxley
Illustrated by Neil Norris
A Winston's Wish publication
Hawthorn Press, 2006
ISBN 978-1-903458-71-6

This is an activity book created to help teenagers remember the person who has died and to help them express their thoughts and feelings. It shows teenagers that remembering is important and necessary – and that it can be fun too.

Michael Rosen's Sad Book
Michael Rosen
Illustrated by Quentin Blake
Walker Books Ltd, 2004
ISBN 978-0744598988

This book is wonderfully honest and will appeal to children and adults of all ages. We all have sad stuff, but what makes Michael Rosen most sad is thinking about his son who died. This book is a simple but emotive story. He talks about what sad is and how it affects him and what he does to cope with it.